WW **kitchen collection**

Chicken

Favourite with a twist
Chicken noodle soup, page 34

Easy midweek dinner
Weekday chicken & 'chips', page 24

Hearty and flavoursome
Chicken & mushroom stroganoff,
page 74

Simple, tasty lunch
Chicken taco salad, page 20

Chicken

The small print

EGGS We use medium eggs, unless otherwise stated. Pregnant women, the elderly and children should avoid recipes with eggs which are raw or not fully cooked.

FRUIT AND VEGETABLES Recipes use medium-size fruit and veg, unless otherwise stated.

LIGHT SOFT CHEESE Where a recipe uses reduced-fat soft cheese, we mean a soft cheese with 30% less fat than its full-fat equivalent.

LOW-FAT SPREAD When a recipe uses a low-fat spread, we mean a spread with a fat content of no more than 39%.

MICROWAVES If we have used a microwave in any of our recipes, the timings will be for an 850-watt microwave oven.

PREP AND COOK TIMES These are approximate and meant to be guidelines only. The prep time includes all the steps up to and following the main cooking time(s). The stated cook times may vary according to your oven.

VEGETARIAN ITALIAN HARD CHEESE Where we reference this in vegetarian recipes, we mean a cheese similar to parmesan (which is not vegetarian) but which is suitable for vegetarians.

GLUTEN FREE Recipes displaying the gluten free icon include ingredients that naturally do not contain gluten, but may also contain processed products, such as sauces, stock cubes and spice mixes. If so, you should ensure that those products do not include any gluten-containing ingredients (wheat, barley or rye) – these will be highlighted in the ingredients list on the product's label. Manufacturers may also indicate whether there is a chance that their product may have been accidentally contaminated with gluten during the manufacturing process. For more information and guidance on gluten-free products, visit www.coeliac.org.uk

SMARTPOINTS have been calculated using the values for generic foods, not brands (except where stated). Tracking using branded items may affect the recorded SmartPoints.

Seven c3

Produced by Seven Publishing on behalf of Weight Watchers International, Inc. Published May 2017. All rights reserved. No part of this publication may be reproduced, stored in a retrieval system or transmitted in any form by any means, electronic, mechanical photocopying, recording or otherwise, without the prior written permission of Seven Publishing.

First published in Great Britain by Seven Publishing Ltd. Copyright © 2017, Weight Watchers International, Inc.

Seven Publishing Ltd
3-7 Herbal Hill
London
EC1R 5EJ
www.seven.co.uk

This book is copyright under the Berne Convention. No reproduction without permission. All rights reserved.

10 9 8 7 6 5 4 3 2 1

Weight Watchers SmartPoints and the SmartPoints icon are the registered trademarks of Weight Watchers International, Inc and are used under license by Weight Watchers (UK) Ltd. All rights reserved.

A CIP catalogue record for this book is available from the British Library. ISBN: 978-0-9935835-6-8

Weight Watchers Publications Team Imogen Prescott, Samantha Rees, Nicola Kirk, Stephanie Williams, Ruby Bamford

PHOTOGRAPHY Ria Osborne. ADDITIONAL PHOTOGRAPHY Tony Briscoe, Jonathan Kennedy, Kris Kirkham, John Paul Urizar

RECIPES & FOOD STYLING Sarah Cook. ADDITIONAL STYLING Sarah Anderson, Anna Crane, Catherine Hill, Bianca Nice, Tracy Rutherford, Vicki Smallwood, Penny Stephens, Polly Webb Wilson

PROP STYLING Tonia Shuttleworth. ADDITIONAL STYLING Stella Kwok, Linda Berlin, Luis Peral

For Seven Publishing Ltd

Editorial & DESIGN
Editor-in-Chief Helen Renshaw
Editor Ward Hellewell Sub editor Chloe Hay
Art director Liz Baird Picture editor Carl Palmer

FOOD TEAM
Food editor Sarah Akhurst Food team manager Linzi Brechin
Senior food assistant Nadine Brown Food assistant Gabriella English
Nutritionist Alexandra Harris

Account management
Account manager Gina Cavaciuti
Publishing consultant Linda Swidenbank
Business director, retail Andy Roughton
Group publishing director Kirsten Price

Production
Production director Sophie Dillon
Colour reproduction by F1 Colour Printed in the UK by CPI Colour

Contents

8   Introduction

10   Top tips for cooking chicken

12   Quick & easy

46   Classics

80   Weekend meals

112   Index

114   SmartPoints index

Healthy, versatile, easy to cook

and loved by just about everyone (including kids!), it's not surprising that chicken regularly tops the list of Britain's *favourite ingredients*.

As well as being a good source of *protein*, chicken has less saturated fat than most other meats, especially when eaten without its skin, so it's great as part of a *healthy-eating plan*.

There's no shortage of ways to turn a simple chicken breast or thigh fillet into a delicious meal – whether it's a simple stir-fry, a spicy curry or a colourful salad. And for a classic family dinner, what could beat a *wonderfully succulent* roast chicken?

In this book from the WW Kitchen Collection, you'll find loads of *brilliant recipes* in which chicken plays the starring role – from quick and easy soups and salads, to those all-time chicken classics and some more adventurous recipes to try out at the weekend.

Each one has been *tried and tested*, and we've worked out all the SmartPoints, making it easy for you to fit them into your eating plan.

LOOK OUT FOR THE SYMBOLS BELOW:

 The number inside the SmartPoints coin tells you how many SmartPoints are in the serving.

⊙ If you're following No Count, you can eat this recipe to your satisfaction without having to count it.

GF A recipe that is totally gluten free, or can be made gluten free with a few simple swaps (see page 6).

✳ Indicates a recipe that is suitable for freezing (without garnishes or side dishes).

for cooking chicken

Not only is chicken versatile, it's quick and easy to cook. Try these top tips to help make it even simpler.

Buy skinless

Using skinless chicken lowers the fat content of your meals, and lowers the SmartPoints value, too. It can be cheaper to buy thighs and drumsticks with the skin on, but just remember to allow an extra 5 minutes prep time to remove it before cooking.

Don't wash it

Washing raw chicken can spread any nasty bacteria that may be on the meat around your kitchen in the water droplets that splash off of it. So don't ever be tempted to wash raw chicken – if you cook it properly, any bacteria that may be on it will be killed.

Go against the grain

If you want to slice your chicken before cooking it, make sure you're slicing against the grain, or across the chicken breast in the direction that will produce shorter strips. All meat – including chicken – is made up of bundles of tough muscle fibres, and cutting those fibres apart will produce a more tender piece of cooked chicken.

Butterfly breast fillets

Chicken breasts are thicker at one end, which means that they may cook unevenly. Butterflying it will solve this problem – slice horizontally through the fillet, starting at the thick end, but don't cut all the way through. Open out the fillet, sandwich it between two pieces of cling film and lightly pound to an even thickness, then grill or pan fry.

Boost flavour

Chicken, especially breast fillet, has quite a delicate flavour, so give it a bit of help with a marinade or spice rub. Marinating can also help break down the fibres in the chicken, which means your cooked chicken breast will be more tender, as well as tastier.

Protect your meat

Chicken breast is such a lean cut that it can be tricky to cook without it turning out dry and tasteless. But a single piece of baking paper placed over the chicken whilst it's in the oven, acts almost like the chicken's missing skin, protecting it and preventing it from drying out.

Give it a rest

Though we often remember to rest a roast or whole bird before carving it, most of us don't allow smaller cuts of meat or poultry to rest before slicing them. Let cooked chicken breast sit for 5-10 minutes before serving; this allows the juices to redistribute themselves throughout the meat, making it juicier.

Use up leftovers

Leftover cooked chicken will keep in the fridge for 3-4 days. Let the chicken cool on the worktop for at least an hour before putting in the fridge in a sealed container or zip-lock bag. When reheating, make sure it's piping hot in the middle before serving and do not reheat more than once.

Freeze it

If you've got leftover chicken you want to freeze, try shredding it then putting it in freezer bags. Shredding makes it easier and quicker to defrost and reheat later. Make sure you let the cooked chicken cool completely before putting it in the freezer.

Choosing your chicken

Everyone has their favourite cut of chicken – some love the lean, white meat of the breast; while others prefer the dark, tender meat of the thigh. Here's a guide to help you choose…

Whole bird

Buying a whole bird is often the cheapest option for feeding a family or a group of friends. Of course a whole bird makes for a perfect roast dinner, but it's also great marinated in a piri-piri rub and served with baked potatoes and salad. Only one or two of you to feed? You can still cook a whole chicken and use the leftovers to make other dishes, such as a quick curry, soup or warm chicken salad.

Breast fillets

The most popular cut of chicken in the UK, breast fillets are also the most versatile. They can be cooked almost any way you like – roasted, fried, grilled, steamed or poached. Use them in curries, fajitas, stir-fries, stews, casseroles, tray bakes and pasta dishes, or as a substitute for burgers. However you like to prepare them, be careful not to overcook breast fillets as the meat can easily become tough and dry.

Thighs

A great cut for using in casseroles, curries and stews; chicken thighs absorb flavours well and stay tender even after long cooking periods, as long as they're cooked in a sauce or broth. They're also great substitutes for drumsticks in tray bakes and are delicious when marinated and barbecued, too. They do have a bit more fat on them than breast fillets, so trim it off before cooking them.

Drumsticks

Drumsticks are a great budget option and so simple to cook. Perfect in tray bakes, on barbecues, in slow cookers and grilled, they're a hugely versatile cut and leftover drumsticks make great lunchbox additions, too. Buy skinless legs or remove the skin yourself to save on SmartPoints, then marinate in your favourite spice rub or sauce in the fridge for a few hours (or overnight) before cooking.

Mini fillets

Sometimes called chicken tenders or chicken fingers, mini fillets are the small strip of meat on the underside of the chicken breast. They're great for making stir fries, kebabs and goujons, but because the meat is thinner than a whole chicken breast, they'll cook more quickly, so take care not to overcook them. They're especially useful if you don't want to use a whole chicken breast in a recipe.

Wings

Many people's favourite cut of chicken, wings offer little morsels of tender and flavoursome meat. Best marinated overnight and then oven-baked, grilled or barbecued, they make great canapés or finger food at parties. Like thighs, chicken wings have more fat than the breast fillet, so remove the skin and trim off as much fat as you can – or save them for an occasional treat!

14 Chipotle chicken club sandwich
16 Chicken Caesar pasta salad
18 Thai chicken wrap
20 Chicken taco salad
22 Chicken patties with Thai salad
24 Weekday chicken & 'chips'
26 Beetroot, chicken & orange salad
28 Chicken laksa
30 Morrocan chicken & couscous salad
32 Chicken burger with blue cheese
34 Chicken noodle soup
36 Chicken & cannellini bean salad
38 Ginger chicken, fennel & apple salad
40 Leek & potato soup with chicken
42 Chicken & broccoli stir-fry
44 Chicken sausage panzanella

Chipotle chicken club sandwich

Serves 1

Prep time
5 minutes

Cook time
10 minutes

This easy version of the classic double-decker sandwich is spiced up with salsa and chipotle paste.

Ingredients

100g chicken breast fillet, skinless
10g chipotle paste
3 slices Weight Watchers Soft Malted Danish Bread
1 tablespoon reduced-fat mayonnaise
1 tablespoon tomato salsa
Handful salad leaves
¼ avocado, sliced

1 Preheat the grill to medium-high. Coat the chicken breast with the chipotle paste and grill for 10 minutes, turning once, until cooked through. Set aside to rest for a few minutes.

2 Toast the bread until golden, then spread the mayonnaise over 2 of the slices.

3 Slice the cooked chicken and sandwich between the 2 slices of toast with the mayonnaise. Spoon the tomato salsa onto the top of the sandwich, then add the salad leaves and sliced avocado. Top with the final piece of toast and cut in half to serve.

SmartPoints
9 per serving

Chicken Caesar pasta salad

Serves 4

Prep time
15 minutes

Cook time
10-12 minutes

This classic Caesar salad is made more substantial by adding wholewheat pasta.

Ingredients

4 x 125g chicken breast fillets, skinless
1 tablespoon olive oil
200g wholewheat fusilli
50g anchovy fillets, drained and chopped
200g cherry tomatoes, halved
150g cucumber, roughly chopped
100g Little Gem lettuce leaves, roughly torn
80ml reduced-fat Caesar dressing
15g parmesan cheese, shaved

1 Put the chicken breast fillets between 2 pieces of cling film and beat with a rolling pin until completely flattened.

2 Put a frying pan or griddle pan over a medium heat. Rub the chicken with the olive oil and cook for 5 minutes on each side, or until cooked through. You may need to do this in batches. Remove from the pan and cut into thick strips.

3 Meanwhile, bring a pan of water to the boil and cook the pasta until al dente. Drain and cool under cold running water.

4 In a bowl, toss the pasta with the chicken, anchovies, tomatoes, cucumber and lettuce. Drizzle over the dressing and serve garnished with the parmesan shavings.

SmartPoints
9 per serving

Thai chicken wrap

Serves 2

Prep time
15 minutes + marinating

Cook time
10-15 minutes

Marinating the chicken before grilling it gives it loads of flavour, and keeps the meat lovely and moist.

Ingredients
165g chicken breast fillet, skinless, cut into strips
½ small carrot, peeled and coarsely grated
¼ cucumber, halved, deseeded and sliced
Juice of ½ lime
2 x 40g tortilla wraps
100g young leaf spinach
1 teaspoon reduced-fat mayonnaise

For the marinade
1 green chilli, deseeded and sliced
2 shallots, chopped
2cm piece fresh ginger, peeled and chopped
1 garlic clove
1 stalk lemon grass, outer layer removed, chopped
Small bunch fresh coriander
Juice and zest of 1 lime
1 kaffir lime leaf
1 teaspoon fish sauce
2 teaspoons olive oil

1 Make the marinade. Put all the marinade ingredients in a blender or mini food processor and blitz until you have a thick paste, then transfer to a medium bowl. Add the chicken and stir to coat in the marinade. Cover with cling film and chill in the fridge for 30 minutes.

2 Meanwhile, in a small bowl, combine the grated carrot with cucumber and lime juice, then set aside.

3 Preheat the grill to medium and line a baking sheet with foil. Put the chicken on the baking sheet and grill for 10-15 minutes, turning occasionally, until cooked through. Set aside.

4 Warm the wraps to pack instructions, then divide the spinach between them. Top with the carrot and cucumber mixture, followed by the chicken. Tightly wrap the tortillas, folding in the ends and sealing them with the mayonnaise to make a secure pocket.

SmartPoints
6 per serving

Chicken taco salad

Serves 1

Prep time
10 minutes

Cook time
7 minutes

A colourful, fresh-tasting salad with a zingy lime dressing and added crunch from the taco shell.

Ingredients
15g corn taco shell
1 tablespoon half-fat créme fraîche
1 tablespoon fresh coriander, chopped
2 teaspoons lime juice
80g cooked skinless chicken breast, sliced
2 iceberg lettuce leaves, torn
½ small red onion, sliced
1 tomato, chopped
2 tablespoons tinned sweetcorn, drained
¼ avocado, chopped

1 Preheat the oven to 160°C, fan 140°C, gas mark 3 and heat the taco shell for 6-7 minutes, or to pack instructions, then break into 3cm-long pieces.

2 Meanwhile, in a small jug, whisk together the créme fraîche, chopped coriander and lime juice, then season and set aside.

3 In a serving bowl, combine the sliced cooked chicken breast, taco pieces, lettuce, red onion, tomato, sweetcorn and avocado. Drizzle with the dressing to serve.

SmartPoints
10 per serving

See page 6

Chicken patties with Thai salad

A simple but tasty noodle salad, served with fragrant chicken patties that you can enjoy hot or cold.

Serves 4

Prep time
15 minutes + chilling

Cook time
10 minutes

Ingredients
Calorie controlled cooking spray
4 tablespoons sweet chilli sauce, to serve

For the patties
350g chicken breast fillets, skinless
4 spring onions, trimmed and roughly chopped
2 tablespoons fresh coriander, chopped
Pinch dried chilli flakes
2 garlic cloves, crushed
2cm-piece fresh ginger, grated
1 tablespoon dark soy sauce
Juice of 1 lime

For the noodle salad
3 nests Thai rice noodles (approx.180g)
½ x 300g bag ready prepared stir-fry vegetables
2 tablespoons fresh coriander, chopped
1 teaspoon toasted sesame oil

1 First make the patties. Put all the ingredients in a food processor or blender and pulse until everything is chopped finely and well combined, but not completely smooth. Chill the mixture in the fridge for 30 minutes.

2 Make the noodle salad by putting the noodles in a bowl and covering with boiling water. Leave for 5 minutes, then drain well and place in a serving bowl. Add the stir-fry vegetables, coriander and sesame oil, then toss to combine.

3 Take the chicken mixture and use your hands to mould it into 12 patties. Heat a nonstick frying pan and mist with cooking spray. Add the patties and gently fry for 6-7 minutes, turning once, until they are cooked through and golden brown.

4 Serve the patties either warm or cold with the noodle salad, and drizzle over the chilli sauce.

SmartPoints
7 per serving

Weekday chicken & 'chips'

Serves 2

Prep time
15 minutes

Cook time
40 minutes

An all-in-one traybake that makes a fast, faff-free meal, perfect for busy weeknights.

Ingredients

Calorie controlled cooking spray
200g new potatoes, scrubbed and sliced into 5mm-thick rounds
1 small onion, cut into wedges
2 x 150g chicken breast fillets, skinless
6 small bay leaves
1 small red pepper, deseeded and sliced into strips
6 baby plum tomatoes
2 garlic cloves, unpeeled
Few fresh thyme sprigs
2 tablespoons reduced-fat mayonnaise
½ teaspoon harissa paste
1 teaspoon lemon juice

1 Preheat the oven to 200°C, fan 180°C, gas mark 6. Mist a roasting tin with cooking spray, add the potatoes and onion in a single layer, then mist again with cooking spray. Put in the preheated oven while you brown the chicken.

2 Heat a nonstick frying pan over a medium heat and mist with cooking spray. Add the chicken fillets and cook for 5 minutes, turning once, until golden. Remove from the pan and make three slashes diagonally on the top of each fillet. Put a bay leaf in each cut.

3 Remove the roasting tin from the oven, turn the potatoes and arrange the pepper, tomatoes and garlic on top. Scatter over the thyme sprigs then lay the chicken fillets on top of the veg. Season to taste.

4 Roast for a further 20 minutes, then remove the garlic cloves and set aside. Roast the chicken and veg for another 5-10 minutes, or until the potatoes are golden and the chicken is cooked through.

5 Meanwhile, squeeze the garlic cloves from their skins into a small bowl and mash with a fork. Stir in the mayonnaise, harissa paste and lemon juice.

6 Remove the bay leaves and thyme sprigs from the tin and discard. Serve the chicken and vegetables with a spoonful of the garlic mayonnaise on the side.

SmartPoints
5 per serving

See page 6

Beetroot, chicken & orange salad

Serves 2

Prep time
15 minutes

Cook time
10 minutes

Orange and beetroot are a great combination and go perfectly with griddled chicken in this simple salad.

Ingredients
2 x 165g chicken breast fillets, skinless
Calorie controlled cooking spray
1 tablespoon extra virgin olive oil
1 tablespoon cider vinegar
1 orange, peeled and segmented, plus juice of ½ an orange
1 teaspoon honey
70g lamb's lettuce
2 large raw beetroots, peeled and spiralised
15g chopped hazelnuts

1 Put the chicken breast fillets between two sheets of cling film and use a rolling pin to flatten them.

2 Heat a griddle pan and mist with cooking spray, then griddle the chicken for 4-5 minutes on each side, or until cooked through. Remove from the pan and set aside to rest for a few minutes, then cut into thick slices.

3 Meanwhile, make the dressing by whisking together the olive oil, cider vinegar, orange juice and honey in a small jug.

4 Put the lamb's lettuce, beetroot and orange into a large bowl, and drizzle over the dressing. Season to taste and toss to combine. Serve the salad topped with the chicken and chopped hazelnuts.

SmartPoints
7 per serving

See page 6

Chicken laksa

Serves 4

Prep time
10 minutes

Cook time
10 minutes

Using pre-cooked chicken breasts in this spicy Malaysian soup makes it really quick to make.

Ingredients

1 teaspoon sunflower oil
1½ tablespoons laksa paste (see tip)
625ml chicken stock, made with 1 stock cube
400ml tin reduced-fat coconut milk
2 cooked chicken breasts, skinless, thinly sliced
200g pak choi
200g dried rice vermicelli noodles
100g fresh bean sprouts
Handful fresh mint leaves
Handful fresh coriander leaves
1 red chilli, deseeded and finely sliced

1 Heat the sunflower oil in a large pan over a medium heat. Add the laksa paste and cook, stirring, for 30 seconds or until fragrant. Add the stock and coconut milk, bring to a gentle simmer and cook for 2 minutes. Then add the chicken and pak choi and cook for a further 2 minutes, or until the chicken is heated through.

2 Meanwhile, prepare the rice noodles to pack instructions or until just tender. Drain.

3 Divide the laksa between 4 serving bowls then top with the rice noodles, bean sprouts, mint, coriander and chilli just before serving.

SmartPoints
12 per serving

See page 6

Tip
Laksa pastes vary in heat, so adjust the amount used according to your taste.

Serves 2

Prep time
20 minutes

Cook time
5-8 minutes

Moroccan chicken & couscous salad

Full of fragrant flavours, this Moroccan-inspired salad could hardly be simpler.

Ingredients

1 small courgette, sliced
50g couscous
100g roasted red peppers (not in oil), drained
100g tinned chickpeas, drained and rinsed
1 teaspoon Moroccan seasoning
Handful fresh coriander leaves
120g cooked skinless chicken breast, sliced
2 tablespoons low-fat baba ganoush

1 Put the courgette slices in a steamer and cook for 5-8 minutes or until tender. Alternatively, put in a microwave-proof dish, cover and microwave on high for 5 minutes. Set aside.

2 Put the couscous in a bowl and pour over enough boiling water to just cover it. Cover with cling film and set aside for 10 minutes, then uncover and fluff up the grains with a fork.

3 In a serving bowl, combine the cooked couscous, sliced courgette, red peppers, chickpeas, Moroccan seasoning and coriander leaves. Season to taste.

4 Top with the sliced chicken breast and the baba ganoush, then serve.

SmartPoints
8 per serving

Tip
Different brands of baba ganoush vary greatly in fat content. We used Sabra Baba Ganoush.

Chicken burger with blue cheese

Serves 4

Prep time
15 minutes

Cook time
12 minutes

These juicy chicken burgers are packed with flavour, and make a nice change from the usual beef burgers.

Ingredients

Calorie controlled cooking spray
3 tablespoons barbecue sauce
1½ teaspoons Tabasco sauce
500g chicken mince
4 shallots, peeled and finely sliced
50g celery, cooked and finely chopped
30g dried breadcrumbs
2 garlic cloves, crushed
4 soft white bread rolls, halved
½ lettuce, shredded
1 tomato, sliced
40g Stilton, crumbled

1 Mist a griddle or nonstick frying pan with cooking spray and put over a medium-high heat. Combine the barbecue sauce and Tabasco sauce in a small bowl and set aside.

2 Put the chicken mince, 1 tablespoon of the barbecue sauce mixture, the shallots, celery, breadcrumbs and garlic in a bowl. Season and mix well, then using wet hands, form the mixture into 4 x 1cm-thick patties. Brush the tops of the patties with half of the remaining sauce mixture.

3 Put the patties in the griddle pan, sauce side down, and brush the other side with the sauce. Cook for 5 minutes on each side or until cooked through. Remove and keep warm.

4 Lightly toast the rolls in the pan. Assemble the burgers using the toasted rolls, lettuce, tomato, patties and Stilton.

SmartPoints
9 per serving

Chicken noodle soup

Serves 4

Prep time
10 minutes

Cook time
15 minutes

A classic soup gets an Asian twist, with the addition of star anise, ginger, soy, chilli and soba noodles.

Ingredients

2 spring onions, trimmed
and cut into 7cm lengths
4 x 125g chicken
breast fillets, skinless
3 whole star anise
30g fresh ginger, grated
270g dried soba noodles
100g oyster mushrooms,
thinly sliced
200g mange tout,
halved diagonally
80ml reduced-salt soy sauce
80g young leaf spinach
Handful fresh
coriander leaves
1 fresh red chilli, deseeded
and finely sliced

1 Put the spring onions, chicken, star anise and ginger in a large pan with 2 litres of water. Put over a medium-high heat and bring to a gentle simmer. Cook, uncovered, for 10 minutes or until the chicken is just cooked through. Remove the chicken from the broth, shred and set aside.

2 In a separate pan, prepare the noodles to pack instructions or until just tender. Drain.

3 Meanwhile, line a fine sieve with a double layer of kitchen towel and put over a medium pan. Strain the broth into the pan, discarding any solids, and bring to the boil.

4 Add the mushrooms, mange tout and shredded chicken. Reduce the heat and simmer for 1-2 minutes or until the vegetables are just tender and the chicken is heated through. Stir in the soy sauce.

5 Divide the spinach and noodles between serving bowls. Ladle over the hot soup and top with the coriander and chilli.

SmartPoints
9 per serving

Chicken & cannellini bean salad

Serves 2

Prep time
10 minutes

Cook time
8-10 minutes

A lovely, Italian-style salad with griddled chicken that's ready in less than half an hour.

Ingredients
Calorie controlled cooking spray
2 x 125g chicken breast fillets, skinless, cut into strips
400g tin cannellini beans, rinsed and drained
½ red onion, finely sliced
250g cherry tomatoes, chopped
Handful fresh flat-leaf parsley, chopped
2 teaspoons extra virgin olive oil
Juice of 1 lemon
Pinch of smoked paprika

1 Heat a griddle or nonstick frying pan over a medium-high heat and mist with the cooking spray. Griddle the chicken for 8-10 minutes, turning every now and then, or until cooked through. Remove from the heat and set aside to rest.

2 Put the cannellini beans in a large bowl, then add the red onion, cherry tomatoes, parsley and cooked chicken. Toss to combine.

3 In a small bowl, whisk together the olive oil, lemon juice and smoked paprika. Drizzle over the salad, season and toss to combine, then serve.

SmartPoints
6 per serving

See page 6

Ginger chicken, fennel & apple salad

Serves 4

Prep time
15 minutes

Cook time
12 minutes

This fresh-tasting salad is packed with flavour and crunch – and looks amazing!

Ingredients
4 x 125g chicken breast fillets, skinless
2 red apples
2 tablespoons lemon juice
1 fennel bulb
2 celery sticks, sliced
½ iceberg lettuce, shredded
25g pecans, chopped, to garnish

For the dressing
5cm piece fresh ginger, peeled and finely grated
1 teaspoon clear honey
80ml buttermilk
2 tablespoons reduced-fat mayonnaise

1 Put the chicken in a pan of boiling water. Reduce the heat to low and poach for 12 minutes, or until cooked through. Transfer to a plate to cool.

2 Meanwhile, make the dressing. Squeeze the ginger over a small bowl, to extract the juice (discard the pulp). Whisk in the honey, then the buttermilk and mayonnaise. Season to taste.

3 Core and quarter the apples, thinly slice, then toss with the lemon juice. Finely slice the fennel, reserving the fronds. Shred the chicken breast fillets, then toss with the celery, fennel, lettuce and apple. Arrange the mixture on a serving platter and drizzle with the dressing, then serve garnished with the pecans and fennel fronds.

SmartPoints
4 per serving

See page 6

Serves 4

Prep time
10 minutes

Cook time
25 minutes

Leek & potato soup with chicken

A warming soup that's great on a chilly day. It freezes well, so you can batch cook it and keep for later.

Ingredients

Calorie controlled
cooking spray
2 leeks, trimmed and
finely sliced
200g potatoes, cubed
1 onion, finely chopped
¼ teaspoon dried rosemary
600ml vegetable stock,
made with 1 stock cube
175g chicken breast
fillet, skinless
300ml skimmed milk
2 teaspoons snipped
fresh chives

1 Mist a large pan with cooking spray and gently sauté the leeks, potatoes and onion for 10 minutes or until softened. Add the rosemary, stock and chicken breast. Cover and leave to simmer for 15 minutes.

2 Remove the chicken from the pan and set aside to keep warm. Transfer the soup to a blender or food processor and blend for about 20 seconds, or until smooth. Return to the pan, stir in the milk and gently heat through, until piping hot. Season to taste.

3 Finely shred the chicken and divide between four warm soup bowls. Ladle the soup over the chicken and sprinkle over the chives to serve.

SmartPoints
3 per serving

✳ GF

See page 6

Chicken & broccoli stir-fry

Serves 2

Prep time
10 minutes

Cook time
10-15 minutes

Use wholewheat noodles in this quick and easy stir-fry to keep you fuller for longer.

Ingredients

100g wholewheat noodles
150g broccoli, sliced
Calorie controlled cooking spray
175g chicken breast fillets, skinless, cut into strips
150g mushrooms, sliced
2cm piece fresh ginger, cut into fine matchsticks
1 large garlic clove, chopped
2 spring onions, sliced
2 tablespoons oyster sauce
1 tablespoon soy sauce

1 Bring a pan of water to the boil, add the noodles and cook for 2 minutes, then add the broccoli and cook for a further 2 minutes to soften. Drain and refresh under cold water.

2 Mist a large wok with cooking spray, add the chicken and mushrooms, and season to taste. Stir-fry for 4 minutes, or until the chicken is almost cooked through and the mushrooms have softened. Stir through the ginger, garlic and spring onions for 1-2 minutes, then add the oyster sauce, soy sauce, noodles and broccoli. Stir-fry for a couple more minutes to heat the noodles and broccoli, then serve.

SmartPoints
8 per serving

Serves 4

Prep time
15 minutes

Cook time
6-8 minutes

Chicken sausage panzanella

A delicious way to use chicken sausages, this Italian-style salad is packed with fresh veggies.

Ingredients
Calorie controlled
cooking spray
450g extra-lean
chicken sausages
4 tomatoes, chopped
1 large cucumber, chopped
2 red peppers, deseeded
and chopped
2 celery sticks, thinly sliced
½ red onion, thinly sliced
12 fresh basil leaves, torn
2 tablespoons
red wine vinegar
1 tablespoon extra virgin
olive oil
4 x 40g slices ciabatta
bread, toasted and torn
into chunks

1 Mist a nonstick frying pan with cooking spray and preheat over a medium-high heat. Add the sausages and cook, turning, for 6-8 minutes or until cooked through. Slice thickly.

2 Put the tomato, cucumber, red peppers, celery, onion and basil in a large bowl.

3 Whisk the vinegar and oil in a small jug, and season to taste.

4 Add the chunks of ciabatta and the sliced sausages to the salad. Pour over the dressing and toss gently to combine, then serve immediately.

SmartPoints
6 per serving

48 Ultimate zesty roast chicken
50 Teriyaki chicken
52 Chicken & leek pie
54 Chicken tikka masala
56 Tex-Mex chicken schnitzel
58 Chicken Florentine pasta
60 Speedy Thai green chicken curry
62 Coq au vin
64 Chicken chow mein
66 Jerk chicken with Caribbean beans
68 Southern baked chicken
70 Paella with chicken, seafood & chorizo
72 Chicken casserole with herb dumplings
74 Chicken & mushroom stroganoff
76 Chicken korma
78 Chicken arrabiata

Ultimate zesty roast chicken

Serves 6

Prep time
15 minutes
+ marinating + resting
Cook time
1 hour 15 minutes

Add tonnes of flavour to your roast chicken with a fresh herb and lime rub.

Ingredients
2kg whole chicken
Calorie controlled cooking spray

For the marinade & sauce
250ml buttermilk
Large handful fresh basil leaves
Large handful fresh flat-leaf parsley leaves
Small handful fresh mint leaves
Zest and juice of 1 lime

For the vegetables
750g new potatoes, larger ones halved
6 garlic cloves, skin left on
½ tablespoon olive oil
Steamed green vegetables, to serve

1 Make the marinade and sauce. Put all the ingredients in a blender and whizz until smooth. Season well. Set aside half the mixture for the sauce and keep chilled in the fridge until needed, the other half will be the marinade.

2 Trim any excess fat from the chicken and put the chicken in a large, non-metallic bowl. Starting at the neck end, carefully lift the skin from the chicken, being careful not to tear it. Pour the marinade under the skin and over the chicken, so that it's well coated. Cover with cling film and refrigerate for at least 4 hours or preferably overnight.

3 Preheat the oven to 200°C, fan 180°C, gas mark 6. Lift the chicken from the bowl, scraping off any excess marinade, and transfer to a large roasting tin. Mist the chicken with cooking spray and season well. Roast for 1 hour 15 minutes, basting every 30 minutes, until cooked through. Leave to rest for 20 minutes before carving.

4 Meanwhile put the new potatoes and garlic in a separate roasting tin and drizzle over the olive oil, then season. Roast alongside the chicken for the final 40 minutes of cooking time. When the potatoes are cooked, squeeze the garlic from the skins and toss with the potatoes to coat. Serve the chicken with the potatoes, reserved sauce and some steamed green vegetables. SmartPoints are based on 80g chicken breast, with equal servings of potatoes and reserved sauce.

SmartPoints
5 per serving

See page 6

Teriyaki chicken

Serves 4

Prep time
10 minutes + marinating
Cook time
12-15 minutes

A delicious Japanese-style stir-fry of marinated chicken, asparagus and spring onions.

Ingredients
4 tablespoons teriyaki marinade
1 tablespoon light soy sauce
½ teaspoon toasted sesame oil
500g chicken breast fillets, skinless, cut into strips
2 teaspoons sesame seeds
Calorie controlled cooking spray
250g asparagus tips
3cm piece fresh ginger, finely chopped
2 spring onions, trimmed and sliced on the diagonal

1 In a shallow dish, mix together the teriyaki marinade, soy sauce and sesame oil. Add the chicken and stir until coated, then cover and put in the fridge to marinate for 30 minutes.

2 Meanwhile, put the sesame seeds in a dry wok or nonstick frying pan and dry fry for about 3 minutes over a medium heat, shaking the pan occasionally, until light golden. Tip the seeds into a small bowl and set aside.

3 Remove the chicken from the marinade (reserving the marinade for later) and mist with cooking spray. Put in the pan and stir-fry for 5-6 minutes until light golden all over. Remove from the pan and set aside.

4 Mist the pan with cooking spray and stir-fry the asparagus for 3 minutes, then add the ginger, chicken and the reserved marinade. Stir-fry for a further 1-2 minutes until the sauce has reduced and thickened. Serve sprinkled with the toasted sesame seeds and spring onions.

SmartPoints
4 per serving

See page 6

Tip
Serve with 120g cooked white rice per person, for an extra 5 SmartPoints per serving.

Chicken & leek pie

Serves 6

Prep time
10 minutes

Cook time
1 hour

Chunks of chicken, leek and peas in a creamy tarragon sauce, topped with golden puff pastry.

Ingredients
1 teaspoon olive oil
700g chicken breast fillets, skinless, diced
3 leeks, trimmed and thickly sliced
2 tablespoons plain flour
400ml chicken stock, made with 1 stock cube
2 tablespoons half-fat crème fraîche
1 tablespoon fresh tarragon, chopped
60g frozen peas
1 sheet light puff pastry
Skimmed milk, to glaze

1 Heat the oil in a large pan and cook the chicken over a medium heat for around 5 minutes, or until it turns golden. Add the leeks and cook for a further 2 minutes.

2 Stir in the flour and continue to cook for another minute before gradually adding the stock, stirring continuously. Bring to the boil for 2 minutes, then reduce the heat to a simmer and cook for around 8 minutes until the sauce has thickened. Remove from the heat and leave to cool slightly. Stir in the crème fraîche, tarragon and peas and set aside.

3 Preheat the oven to 200°C, fan 180°C, gas mark 6. Spoon the chicken mixture into a 2-litre pie dish. Unroll the pastry and drape over the top of the pie. Press the edges down to create a seal and trim any excess pastry from around the edges. Make a couple of slits in the top to allow steam to escape, then brush the milk over the pastry.

4 Bake for 25-30 minutes or until the top is crisp and golden.

SmartPoints
10 per serving

Chicken tikka masala

Serves 4

Prep time
15 minutes + marinating

Cook time
30 minutes

This Indian-restaurant classic is served with brown rice and a tomato, onion and cucumber salad.

Ingredients
400g chicken breast fillets, skinless, cubed
200g brown basmati rice
Calorie controlled cooking spray
1 onion, finely chopped
1 tablespoon tikka curry paste
3 garlic cloves, chopped
200g passata
200ml reduced-fat coconut milk
Handful fresh coriander, roughly torn

For the marinade
170g 0% fat natural Greek yogurt
3cm piece fresh ginger, finely grated
4 garlic cloves, crushed
1 tablespoon tikka curry paste

For the salad
4 tomatoes, chopped
1 small red onion, chopped
1 small cucumber, chopped
Juice of ½ lemon

1 Put the marinade ingredients in a shallow dish, season and stir to combine. Add the chicken, stir to coat, then cover and put in the fridge to marinate for 15 minutes.

2 Mix all of the salad ingredients together in a bowl, and set aside.

3 Cook the rice to pack instructions. Meanwhile, preheat a large nonstick frying pan and mist with cooking spray. Remove the chicken from the marinade, reserving the excess, and fry over a medium high heat for around 8 minutes, until lightly charred and just cooked. Set aside.

4 Wipe the pan clean, mist with cooking spray and add the onion. Gently cook for 10 minutes until softened – add a splash of water if it starts to stick. Add the curry paste, garlic and reserved yogurt marinade. Cook for 3 minutes, stirring all the time.

5 Add the passata and coconut milk to the curry and bring almost to the boil. Return the chicken to the pan and simmer for 5 minutes until piping hot. Stir the coriander through the curry and serve with the rice and salad.

Tip
Try serving this with mini naan breads for an extra 3 SmartPoints per naan.

SmartPoints
10 per serving

See page 6

Tex-Mex chicken schnitzel

Serves 4

Prep time
10 minutes

Cook time
10 minutes

Adding taco seasoning to the crumb coating gives these delicious chicken fillets a spicy twist.

Ingredients
2 x 200g chicken breast fillets, skinless
2 tablespoons plain flour
1 egg, lightly beaten
50g panko breadcrumbs
30g pack taco seasoning
1½ tablespoons sunflower oil
500g reduced-fat coleslaw
Lettuce leaves, to serve

1 Cut the chicken breasts horizontally into 2 thin fillets. Using a meat mallet or rolling pin, pound the chicken between 2 pieces of cling film until they're about 4mm thick.

2 Put the flour on a plate. Whisk the egg with 2 teaspoons water in a shallow bowl. Combine the breadcrumbs and taco seasoning on another plate.

3 Coat each chicken fillet in the flour, then the egg mixture and finally the breadcrumb mixture. Set aside.

4 Heat the oil in a large nonstick frying pan over a medium-high heat. Add the schnitzels and cook, in batches, for 2 minutes each side or until golden and cooked through.

5 Serve the schnitzels with the coleslaw and lettuce leaves on the side.

SmartPoints
11 per serving

Chicken Florentine pasta

Serves 4

Prep time
5 minutes

Cook time
15 minutes

Creamy spinach, sun-dried tomatoes and chicken work beautifully together in this tasty pasta dish.

Ingredients
225g wholewheat tagliatelle
1 teaspoon olive oil
1 onion, finely chopped
1 garlic clove,
finely chopped
6 sprigs fresh thyme, leaves
picked and chopped
150g half-fat crème fraîche
Zest of ½ lemon
200g young leaf spinach
75g sun-dried tomatoes,
drained and thinly sliced
300g cooked skinless
chicken breasts, shredded
30g parmesan cheese,
grated, to serve

1 Cook the pasta in a pan of boiling water for 10-12 minutes or until al dente. Drain, reserving a little of the cooking liquid.

2 Meanwhile, heat the oil in a large pan and cook the onion for 5-10 minutes, adding a little water if the onion starts to stick. Add the garlic and thyme for the final minute. Pour in the crème fraîche and continue to cook for 1-2 minutes, then stir through the lemon zest.

3 Put the spinach in a covered dish and microwave on high for 2 minutes to wilt. Add the wilted spinach, sun-dried tomatoes, chicken and pasta to the pan. Stir to combine, adding a little of the reserved cooking water to loosen if needed, until the chicken is heated through.

4 Season with salt and freshly ground black pepper and serve garnished with the parmesan cheese.

SmartPoints
12 per serving

Serves 2

Prep time
5 minutes

Cook time
15 minutes

Speedy Thai green chicken curry

In a hurry? This fragrant, spicy chicken and veg curry cooked in coconut milk is ready in just 20 minutes.

Ingredients

100g white rice
40g Thai green curry paste
200ml reduced-fat coconut milk
75ml chicken stock, made with ¼ stock cube
200g cooked mixed vegetables, cut into bite-size pieces
200g chicken breast fillets, skinless, cut into strips
Juice of ½ a lime, plus extra wedges to serve
½ teaspoon Thai fish sauce
Small handful fresh coriander, chopped
1 red chilli, finely sliced

1 Cook the rice to pack instructions.

2 Meanwhile, heat a wok or large nonstick frying pan over a medium heat and add the curry paste. Cook, stirring, for a minute, then stir in the coconut milk and stock.

3 Bring to the boil and add the vegetables. Cook, stirring, for another minute, then add the chicken. Cook for 7-8 minutes, stirring occasionally, until the chicken is cooked through and the veg is tender. Stir in the lime juice and fish sauce.

4 Sprinkle the coriander and chilli over the curry and serve with the rice, with the lime wedges on the side.

SmartPoints
12 per serving

See page 6

Tip
Use whatever veg you like in this recipe – green beans, butternut squash, asparagus and baby corn all work well.

Serves 4

Prep time
15 minutes
Cook time
45-50 minutes

Coq au vin

A classic French dish of chicken, bacon, mushrooms and herbs cooked in a delicious red wine sauce.

Ingredients

2 teaspoons olive oil
4 x 150g chicken thighs, skinless, fat trimmed
80g bacon medallions, chopped
2 onions, cut into thick wedges
2 garlic cloves, chopped
600g button mushrooms, halved
1 tablespoon plain flour
140g tomato paste
250ml chicken stock, made with ½ stock cube
185ml dry red wine
2 fresh or dried bay leaves
4 fresh thyme sprigs, plus extra to serve
Steamed green beans, to serve

1 Heat the oil in a large heavy-bottomed pan over a medium-high heat. Cook the chicken, turning, for 5 minutes or until browned, then transfer to a plate and set aside.

2 Add the bacon, onion and garlic to the pan, and cook, stirring, for 5 minutes or until softened. Add the mushrooms and cook, stirring, for another 5 minutes or until softened.

3 Whisk the flour and tomato paste together in a bowl. Gradually add in the stock and wine, whisking until smooth. Pour into the pan with the mushroom mixture. Return the chicken to the pan and add the bay leaves and thyme sprigs. Bring to a simmer, then reduce the heat to low, and cook, covered, for 25-30 minutes, or until the chicken is cooked through.

4 Sprinkle over the extra thyme and serve with the green beans on the side.

SmartPoints
10 per serving

Tip
Serve this with 150g boiled new potatoes per person, for an extra 3 SmartPoints per serving.

Chicken chow mein

Serves 4

Prep time
15 minutes + marinating

Cook time
15 minutes

Keep dried noodles in your storecupboard for delicious stir-fries like this Chinese-style favourite.

Ingredients

600g chicken breast fillets, skinless, cut into strips
6 tablespoons soy sauce
200g dried egg noodles
Calorie controlled cooking spray
1 large onion, sliced
1 carrot, cut into batons
100g baby corn, halved lengthways
100g sugar snap peas
2 large garlic cloves, finely sliced
3cm piece fresh root ginger, finely chopped
150g Chinese leaves, finely sliced
2 tablespoons Chinese cooking wine or dry sherry
4 tablespoons oyster sauce

1 Put the chicken and 4 tablespoons of the soy sauce into a shallow dish, stir to coat, then cover and put in the fridge to marinate for 30 minutes.

2 Meanwhile, cook the noodles to pack instructions, then drain and refresh under cold running water. Put in a bowl, cover with cold water and set aside.

3 Remove the chicken from the soy sauce and discard the marinade. Heat a large wok or nonstick frying pan over a medium heat, mist with cooking spray and stir-fry the chicken for 4-5 minutes until golden and cooked through. Remove from the pan and set aside.

4 Add the onion, carrot, baby corn and sugar snap peas to the pan, mist with more cooking spray and stir-fry for 3 minutes. Add the garlic, ginger and Chinese leaves, then stir-fry for another minute.

5 Drain the cooked noodles and add to the pan along with the Chinese cooking wine or dry sherry, the remaining soy sauce, the oyster sauce and the chicken, and stir until combined and heated through. Season to taste, then serve.

SmartPoints
8 per serving

Jerk chicken with Caribbean beans

Serves 4

Prep time
15 minutes

Cook time
30 minutes

Spicy griddled chicken is served with beans, peppers and butternut squash on a warm tortilla wrap.

Ingredients

8 x 60g mini chicken breast fillets, skinless
2 tablespoons jerk spice mix
350g butternut squash, peeled, deseeded and cut into 1cm cubes
Calorie controlled cooking spray
1 onion, finely chopped
2 large garlic cloves, finely chopped
1 yellow pepper, deseeded and diced
1 teaspoon dried thyme
1 teaspoon cumin seeds
400g tin black beans, drained and rinsed
3 tablespoons fresh coriander, chopped
25g sweet and hot jalapeños (from a jar), drained and roughly chopped
4 tortilla wraps, to serve
4 tablespoons 0% fat natural Greek yogurt, to serve

1 Put the chicken fillets on a plate, sprinkle over the jerk spices, coating both sides, then cover and chill until needed. Bring a pan of water to the boil, add the butternut squash and cook for about 10 minutes or until tender. Drain, then refresh under cold running water. Set aside.

2 Meanwhile, heat a lidded nonstick pan, mist with cooking spray, then add the onion and cook for 8 minutes, covered, stirring regularly. Add the garlic, pepper, thyme and cumin seeds. Mist with a little more cooking spray and stir-fry for 3 minutes.

3 Preheat the oven to 100°C, fan 90°C, gas mark ¼. Add the black beans, butternut squash, and 2 tablespoons of water to the pan, along with the onions and peppers. Cook for 5 minutes, or until heated through. Stir through the coriander and jalapeños.

4 Wrap the tortillas in foil and warm in the oven. Meanwhile, heat a griddle or nonstick frying pan, mist the chicken with cooking spray and cook four of the chicken fillets for 6 minutes, turning once, or until cooked through. Cover and keep warm while you cook the second batch.

5 Top each tortilla with the black bean mixture, the chicken and a spoonful of yogurt to serve.

SmartPoints
8 per serving

Southern baked chicken

Serves 4

Prep time
15 minutes + marinating

Cook time
30-35 minutes

Ingredients
**4 chicken drumsticks,
skin removed
4 x 125g chicken
thighs, skinless
250ml buttermilk
75g plain flour
1½ tablespoons Cajun
seasoning
Calorie controlled
cooking spray
500g potatoes, peeled
and chopped
2 teaspoons low-fat spread
Lemon wedges, to serve**

In this healthier version of the takeaway favourite, drumsticks and thighs are baked in the oven.

1 Combine the chicken and 185ml of the buttermilk in a shallow dish. Cover and put in the fridge for 3 hours, then drain and discard the buttermilk.

2 Combine the flour and Cajun seasoning on a plate. Toss each piece of chicken in the flour mixture to coat and then put on a tray and chill in the fridge for 15 minutes.

3 Preheat the oven to 240°C, fan 220°C, gas mark 9. Line a large baking sheet with baking paper. Place a wire rack over the prepared tray and lightly mist with cooking spray. Arrange the chicken on the rack in a single layer and lightly mist with more cooking spray. Bake for 15 minutes and then reduce the oven to 220°C, fan 200°C, gas mark 7. Turn the chicken and bake for another 15-20 minutes or until golden and cooked through.

4 Meanwhile, boil, steam or microwave the potatoes until tender. Drain. Mash in a large bowl with the spread and remaining buttermilk until smooth. Season to taste. Serve the chicken and mash with the lemon wedges on the side.

SmartPoints
11 per serving

Tip
Serve with steamed green beans and Savoy cabbage for no extra SmartPoints.

Paella with chicken, seafood & chorizo

Serves 4

Prep time
10 minutes

Cook time
40-45 minutes

Full of delicious Mediterranean flavours, this classic Spanish dish is great for entertaining.

Ingredients

Calorie controlled cooking spray
200g chicken breast fillets, skinless, cut into chunks
1 onion, sliced
1 green pepper, deseeded and sliced
2 garlic cloves, crushed
25g chorizo, diced
175g paella or Arborio rice
400g tin chopped tomatoes with herbs
450ml chicken stock, made with 1 stock cube
250g mixed seafood, frozen or fresh
2 tablespoons fresh parsley, chopped, to serve

1 Mist a large nonstick frying pan with cooking spray and put over a medium heat. Add the chicken and stir-fry for 5 minutes until browned. Remove from the pan and set aside.

2 Mist the pan again with cooking spray, add the onion and pepper and cook for 3 minutes. Add the garlic, chorizo and a splash of water and cook for 2 minutes. Stir in the rice, followed by the tomatoes, stock and chicken. Reduce the heat to a gentle simmer and cook, stirring occasionally, for 25-30 minutes until the rice is just tender.

3 Add the seafood and cook for 5 minutes until hot (it may need a little longer if frozen). Add extra hot water if it gets too dry. Season to taste and scatter over the parsley to serve.

SmartPoints
7 per serving

See page 6

Chicken casserole with herb dumplings

Serves 4

Prep time
20 minutes

Cook time
35 minutes

This warming chicken and veg stew is topped with hearty dumplings that are flavoured with fresh herbs.

Ingredients

200g self-raising flour
100g low-fat spread
1½ tablespoons fresh thyme, chopped
1 tablespoon fresh flat-leaf parsley, chopped
Calorie controlled cooking spray
400g chicken breast fillets, skinless, cubed
2 leeks, trimmed and sliced
2 carrots, chopped
2 parsnips, chopped
2 celery sticks, chopped
2 bay leaves
150ml dry white wine
1 tablespoon wholegrain mustard
1 teaspoon Marmite
550ml chicken stock, made with 1 stock cube
1½ tablespoons cornflour, mixed with 3 tablespoons cold water
Steamed broccoli, to serve

1 In a bowl, rub together the flour, low-fat spread, ½ tablespoon of the thyme and all of the parsley. Season well, then stir in about 4 tablespoons of cold water to form a soft, but not sticky, dough. Roll into equal-size dumplings and set aside.

2 Mist a large lidded nonstick casserole dish with cooking spray. Add the chicken and cook over a high heat for 5 minutes until browned. Remove and set aside. Mist the pan again, stir in the vegetables, remaining thyme and bay leaves and cook for 4 minutes until slightly golden. Add the wine, mustard, Marmite and stock and leave to simmer for 10 minutes.

3 Return the chicken to the pan, stir in the cornflour mixture, season, then place the dumplings on top. Cover and simmer for 15 minutes, until the dumplings are cooked through. Serve with some steamed brocolli on the side.

SmartPoints
13 per serving

Chicken & mushroom stroganoff

Serves 4

Prep time
15 minutes

Cook time
25 minutes

This version of the popular dish uses chicken fillet, cooked in a creamy mushroom sauce.

Ingredients

1½ tablespoons olive oil
500g chicken breast fillets, skinless, thinly sliced
1 onion, finely sliced
2 garlic cloves, crushed
200g chestnut mushrooms, sliced
100g button mushrooms, sliced
2 tablespoons plain flour
1 teaspoon paprika
250ml beef or chicken stock, made with ½ stock cube
1 tablespoon Worcestershire sauce
250g young leaf spinach
2 tablespoons half-fat créme fraîche

1 Heat 2 teaspoons of the oil in a deep, nonstick frying pan over a medium-high heat. Cook the chicken, stirring, for 5 minutes or until browned. Transfer to a plate.

2 Turn the heat down to medium and add another 2 teaspoons of oil to the pan. Cook the onion, stirring, for 5 minutes or until softened. Add the garlic and mushrooms and cook, stirring, for 5 minutes or until the mushrooms are golden and tender.

3 Add the flour and paprika and cook, stirring, for 1 minute or until fragrant. Add the stock and Worcestershire sauce and bring to the boil. Return the chicken to the pan. Reduce the heat and simmer, uncovered, for 5-7 minutes or until the sauce has thickened slightly and the chicken is cooked through.

4 Meanwhile, heat the remaining oil in a large nonstick frying pan over a high heat. Cook the spinach, stirring, for 1-2 minutes or until just wilted.

5 Stir the créme fraîche into the chicken mixture and cook for another minute, or until heated through. Serve the stroganoff with the wilted spinach.

SmartPoints
6 per serving

Tip
Serve with 85g cooked brown rice per person, for an extra 3 SmartPoints per serving.

Chicken korma

Serves 4

Prep time
15 minutes

Cook time
30 minutes

Tender chunks of chicken in a mild sauce – try this healthier version of the much-loved curry.

Ingredients
500g chicken breast fillets, skinless, cubed
200g basmati rice

For the korma sauce
1 teaspoon vegetable oil
1 small onion, diced
1 carrot, diced
1 small apple, peeled, cored and diced
1 tablespoon korma curry paste
2 teaspoons mango chutney
2 teaspoons tomato purée
150ml reduced-fat coconut milk
75ml chicken stock, made with ¼ stock cube

1 For the sauce, heat the oil in a lidded nonstick pan and add the onion and carrot. Cover and cook on a low heat, stirring occasionally, for 15 minutes. Add the apple, cover and cook for another 5 minutes or until everything is soft.

2 Stir in the korma paste, mango chutney and tomato purée, then remove from the heat. Blend in the coconut milk and stock, then whizz to a purée using a stick blender.

3 Add the chicken to the curry sauce and leave to simmer for 10 minutes, or until cooked through. Meanwhile, cook the rice to pack instructions.

4 Serve the curry and rice with some steamed vegetables, such as pak choi or baby corn.

SmartPoints
10 per serving

See page 6

Tip
Any leftover curry will keep in the freezer for up to one month.

Serves 4

Chicken arrabiata

Prep time
15 minutes

Cook time
20 minutes

A popular Italian pasta dish with a spicy tomato sauce – add more dried chilli if you like it hotter!

Ingredients

300g chicken breast fillets, skinless, finely sliced
Zest and juice of ½ lemon
1 garlic clove, crushed
25g pack fresh basil, shredded
300g wholemeal penne pasta
Calorie controlled cooking spray

For the pasta sauce

1 onion, finely chopped
3 garlic cloves, chopped
Good pinch dried chilli flakes, crushed
250g ripe tomatoes, chopped
1 teaspoon tomato purée

1 Combine the chicken, lemon zest and juice, crushed garlic and half of the basil in a small bowl. Season well and set to one side to marinate.

2 Cook the pasta to pack instructions until al dente. Drain and keep warm.

3 Heat a large nonstick frying pan over a medium-high heat and mist with cooking spray. Cook the chicken for 5 minutes, until cooked through. Remove from the pan and set aside.

4 To make the sauce, mist the pan with a little more cooking spray, add the onion and cook for 5 minutes, adding water to prevent it burning if necessary. Add the garlic and chilli and cook for 2 minutes, then add the tomatoes, the tomato purée and 150ml water. Bring to the boil and then simmer for 5 minutes.

5 Add the cooked chicken and pasta to the sauce, season to taste and leave to heat through for 2–3 minutes. Scatter over the remaining basil to serve.

SmartPoints
8 per serving

82 Chicken & vegetable traybake
84 Paprika chicken with lentils
86 Creamy chicken pies
88 Middle Eastern chicken with rice
90 Goat's cheese & pesto stuffed chicken
92 Harissa roast chicken & bulgur wheat
94 Chicken merguez meatballs
96 Roast chicken with chorizo & peppers
98 Chicken & broad bean risotto
100 Balsamic roasted chicken
102 Griddled chicken with herby couscous
104 Chicken pies with roasted vegetables
106 Harissa chicken & chickpea casserole
108 Chicken, mushroom & wild rice pilaf
110 Chicken, lentil & tomato bake

Chicken & vegetable traybake

Serves 4

Prep time
20 minutes

Cook time
1 hour 20 minutes –
1 hour 45 minutes

This easy dish of roasted vegetables and chicken thighs is made extra special with a fruity sauce.

Ingredients

500g Chantenay carrots, halved or quartered if larger
2 red onions, each cut into 8 wedges
2 courgettes, cut into 2cm-thick rounds
2 teaspoons olive oil
30g fresh sage, rosemary and thyme sprigs
8 x 115g chicken thighs, skinless
200g blueberries
1 apple, peeled, cored and diced
1 tablespoon balsamic vinegar
1 teaspoon light brown soft sugar
1 cinnamon stick
2 tablespoons cornflour

1 Preheat the oven to 180°C, fan 160°C, gas mark 4. Toss the vegetables together in a large roasting tin with 1 teaspoon of the oil. Season and scatter over the herbs. Rub the rest of the oil into the chicken thighs and season. Arrange the chicken thighs on top of the veg and herbs, then cover loosely with foil and roast for 30 minutes.

2 Remove the foil and roast for a further 40 minutes until the chicken is golden. Transfer the chicken to a platter, cover with foil and leave to rest. Check the vegetables – if they're still firm, cook for another 10-15 minutes until tender.

3 Meanwhile, put the fruit in a small pan and add the vinegar, sugar and cinnamon. Cover and cook for 10 minutes until the apples are tender and the berries are just beginning to release juice. Discard the cinnamon and mash the fruit to a chunky sauce. Set aside and keep warm.

4 Make the gravy. Strain the juices from the roasting tin into a medium pan. Discard the herbs and arrange the vegetables around the chicken on the platter. Cover with foil to keep warm. Add 250ml of water to the pan of juices and bring to the boil. Bubble for 5 minutes until reduced by half. Mix the cornflour with 250ml water until smooth and then gradually add to the pan, whisking continuously. Cook for 5-6 minutes then season.

5 Serve the chicken and vegetables with the sauce and gravy.

SmartPoints
12 per serving

See page 6

Paprika chicken with lentils

Serves 4

Prep time
20 minutes

Cook time
45 minutes

This lentil and chicken stew is served with lightly spiced, oven roasted vegetables.

Ingredients
500g butternut squash, peeled, deseeded and chopped
1 carrot, chopped
1 courgette, chopped
Calorie controlled cooking spray
1 teaspoon cumin seeds
1 onion, chopped
1 garlic clove, chopped
3 fresh thyme sprigs, leaves picked and chopped
2 spring onions, trimmed and sliced
2 red chillies, chopped
1 teaspoon paprika
300ml passata with basil
200ml chicken stock, made with 1 stock cube
1 portabella mushroom, diced
500g chicken breast fillets, skinless, chopped
40g red lentils, rinsed
Handful fresh flat-leaf parsley, chopped

1 Preheat the oven to 200°C, fan 180°C, gas mark 6. Put the squash, carrot and courgette on a baking sheet and mist with cooking spray. Crush the cumin seeds in a pestle and mortar and sprinkle over the vegetables. Season and toss everything together to combine. Roast for 40-45 minutes, turning halfway.

2 Meanwhile, mist a large pan with cooking spray and cook the onion for 8-10 minutes. Add the garlic, thyme, spring onions, chillies and paprika, and cook for another 2 minutes.

3 Stir in the passata, stock and mushroom. Simmer for 15 minutes, to reduce slightly, then add the chicken and lentils. Cook for another 15 minutes.

4 Season and serve with the roasted veg, garnished with the chopped parsley.

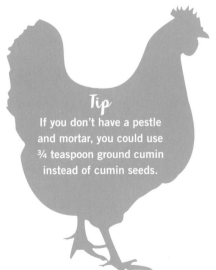

Tip
If you don't have a pestle and mortar, you could use ¾ teaspoon ground cumin instead of cumin seeds.

SmartPoints
2 per serving

See page 6

84

Serves 2

Prep time
15 minutes
Cook time
15 minutes

Creamy chicken pies

This chicken and mash pie is a tasty alternative to a shepherd's pie and still just as comforting.

Ingredients
400g potatoes, cut into
small chunks
125g parsnips, peeled and
cut into small chunks
300g chicken breast fillets,
skinless, cut into
small chunks
1 carrot, finely sliced
250ml chicken stock,
made with ½ stock cube
1 bay leaf
60g sweetcorn,
frozen or tinned
2 teaspoons cornflour
40g low-fat soft cheese
1 tablespoon chopped
fresh flat-leaf parsley

1 Bring a pan of water to the boil. Add the potatoes and parsnips, cover and simmer for 10 minutes until soft. Drain well and mash. Season to taste.

2 Meanwhile, put the chicken, carrot, stock and bay leaf in a pan, bring to the boil and simmer, uncovered, for 6-8 minutes, or until the chicken is cooked. Add the sweetcorn and bring back to the boil.

3 Mix the cornflour with 1 tablespoon water until you have a smooth paste. Stir into the chicken mixture and let it bubble for a minute to thicken, then whisk in the soft cheese and cook gently for another minute until hot. Remove the bay leaf and stir in the parsley.

4 Preheat the grill to medium. Spoon the chicken mixture into individual pie dishes or into a larger ovenproof dish, and top with the mash. Grill for 3-5 minutes until the potato is just golden on top, then serve.

SmartPoints
10 per serving

See page 6

Middle Eastern chicken with rice

Serves 4

Prep time
10 minutes + marinating

Cook time
18-20 minutes

A marinade of yogurt, garlic, ginger and saffron gives this dish loads of flavour and colour.

Ingredients
600g chicken breast fillets, skinless, cubed
200g brown basmati rice
2 teaspoons ground cumin
Handful fresh coriander, roughly chopped

For the marinade
1 large onion, thinly sliced
2 garlic cloves, crushed
3cm piece fresh ginger, grated
70g 0% fat natural Greek yogurt
Juice of 1 lime
Large pinch saffron threads

1 Combine all the marinade ingredients in a shallow dish. Add the chicken pieces, stir to coat, cover and put in the fridge to marinate for at least 4 hours, or overnight if possible.

2 Preheat the oven to 200°C, fan 180°C, gas mark 6. Line 2 baking sheets with baking paper, spoon the chicken and marinade onto them and cook in the oven for 18-20 minutes, or until the chicken pieces are cooked through and browned at the edges.

3 Meanwhile, cook the rice to pack instructions, stirring the cumin through while it cooks. Drain and season to taste.

4 Spoon the rice onto a serving dish, top with the chicken, and sprinkle over the coriander to serve.

SmartPoints
7 per serving

See page 6

Goat's cheese & pesto stuffed chicken

Serves 2

Prep time
10 minutes

Cook time
20-25 minutes

A delicious way to cook a chicken breast fillet – the cheese and pesto creates a tasty sauce.

Ingredients
2 x 165g chicken breast
fillets, skinless
40g goat's cheese
1 tablespoon green pesto
1 lemon
Pinch crushed chillies
2 garlic cloves, skin left on,
squashed with the back
of a knife
50ml dry white wine
2 x 140g sweet potatoes
½ tablespoon balsamic glaze
100g salad leaves

1 Preheat the oven to 200°C, fan 180°C, gas mark 6. Cut a pocket in the thickest part of the chicken breasts and stuff with the cheese and pesto.

2 Put the chicken in a small baking dish. Cut 4 slices from the lemon and put 2 on each chicken breast, then sprinkle over the chillies. Add the garlic, white wine and the juice of the rest of the lemon. Season and cook for 20-25 minutes, or until the chicken is cooked through.

3 Meanwhile, pierce the sweet potatoes with a knife and cook in the microwave for 8-10 minutes until tender. Wrap in foil and finish off in the oven for 5 minutes.

4 Drizzle the balsamic glaze over the salad leaves and serve with the chicken and sweet potatoes.

SmartPoints
10 per serving

See page 6

Harissa roast chicken & bulgur wheat

Serves 6

Prep time
20 minutes + resting

Cook time
1 hour 40 minutes

Warm bulgur wheat with roasted peppers and onions is a perfect match for this spicy roast chicken.

Ingredients

1.75kg whole chicken
2 teaspoons harissa paste
2 lemons, 1 quartered, 1 zested and juiced
3 peppers, deseeded and sliced
2 red onions, cut into wedges
2 teaspoons olive oil
250g bulgur wheat, rinsed well
1 chicken stock cube, mixed with 5 tablespoons boiling water
Handful fresh flat-leaf parsley, finely chopped

1 Heat the oven to 200°C, fan 180°C, gas mark 6. Put the chicken in a roasting tin, then carefully lift the skin away from the breast, starting at the neck end. Rub most of the harissa paste over the breast meat, under the skin, then rub the remainder over the skin of the legs and wings. Replace the skin, squeeze the lemon quarters over, then add to the tin. Roast for 1 hour 40 minutes or until the juices run clear. Loosely cover with foil after about 30 minutes. When cooked, remove from the oven and leave to rest for 20 minutes before removing the skin and discarding. Then carve the meat.

2 Meanwhile, toss the peppers and onions with the oil in a large roasting tin. Roast for 45 minutes alongside the chicken, until softened and charred.

3 Put the bulgur wheat in a bowl, add the chicken stock, then pour over 600ml boiling water. Stir, cover with cling film and leave for 15 minutes, then fluff with a fork. Add the roasted vegetables, lemon zest, juice and parsley, stir to combine, then season to taste. Serve with 120g carved skinless chicken per person. SmartPoints are based on mixed meat.

SmartPoints
8 per serving

Serves 4

Prep time
20 minutes + chilling

Cook time
20 minutes

Chicken merguez meatballs

This tasty meatball and couscous recipe is inspired by merguez – a spicy sausage from North Africa.

Ingredients
4 slices Weight Watchers Sliced Brown Danish Bread
100ml skimmed milk
400g chicken breast fillets, skinless, diced
1 egg, lightly beaten
2 garlic cloves, crushed
1 tablespoon harissa paste
¾ teaspoon ground cumin
1 teaspoon fennel seeds
½ teaspoon ground coriander
Calorie controlled cooking spray
500ml chicken stock, made with 1 stock cube
150g wholewheat giant couscous
2 courgettes, sliced into ribbons
1 red pepper, deseeded and finely sliced
1 red onion, cut into wedges
Juice of 1 lemon, plus a few wedges, to serve
150g 0% fat natural Greek yogurt
3 tablespoons chopped fresh mint, plus a few mint sprigs to garnish

1 Tear the bread into chunks and soak in the milk for 5 minutes. Pulse the chicken in a food processor until roughly chopped. Add the soaked bread, egg, garlic, harissa paste, ½ teaspoon of the cumin, the fennel seeds and ground coriander. Season and process until smooth but retaining some texture.

2 Use your hands to shape the mixture into 20 meatballs and put on a baking sheet lined with baking paper. Chill in the freezer for 20 minutes to firm up.

3 Preheat the oven to 200°C, fan 180°C, gas mark 6. Take the meatballs out of the freezer, mist with cooking spray, then bake for 20 minutes until cooked through and golden.

4 Meanwhile, bring the stock to the boil and add the couscous. Boil for 6-8 minutes, stirring occasionally. Drain and set aside.

5 Heat a griddle pan over a medium-high heat. Put the courgettes, pepper and onion in a large bowl, mist with cooking spray and season well. Griddle for 2 minutes on each side until just charred and tender – you'll need to do this in batches. Toss the veg with the couscous and half the lemon juice.

6 In a small bowl, mix the yogurt with the mint and remaining lemon juice and cumin.

7 Serve the meatballs and couscous garnished with the mint sprigs, with the yogurt and lemon wedges on the side.

SmartPoints
8 per serving

Roast chicken with chorizo & peppers

Serves 4

Prep time
10 minutes

Cook time
50 minutes

Spicy chorizo and olives add lots of flavour to chicken thighs and potatoes in this fuss-free traybake.

Ingredients

300g baby new potatoes
4 garlic cloves, skin left on
500g chicken thighs, skinless, boneless
1 red onion, cut into wedges
½ lemon, cut into 4 wedges
Calorie controlled cooking spray
1 red or yellow pepper, deseeded and sliced
100g cooking chorizo, sliced
20 black olives
100g rocket

1 Preheat the oven to 190°C, fan 170°C, gas mark 5. Put the potatoes in a large roasting tin. Squash the garlic cloves with the flat part of a knife and put them in the tin. Add the chicken along with the onion and lemon wedges. Season everything and mist well with cooking spray. Bake for 25 minutes.

2 Add the pepper, chorizo and olives to the tin and return to the oven for a further 25 minutes, or until everything is cooked. Serve with the rocket.

SmartPoints
11 per serving

See page 6

Tip
Bulk out this dish by serving it with some steamed green beans or broccoli on the side.

Chicken & broad bean risotto

Serves 4

Prep time
10 minutes

Cook time
30-35 minutes

This risotto is simple to make but has loads of flavour – it's perfect for a weekend family meal.

Ingredients

Calorie controlled cooking spray
300g chicken breast fillets, skinless, cut into small chunks
250g Arborio rice
4 spring onions, trimmed and chopped
1 garlic clove, crushed
100ml dry white wine
850ml hot vegetable stock, made with 1 stock cube
75g frozen broad beans, defrosted
2 tablespoons grated parmesan cheese
Fresh basil leaves, to garnish

1 Mist a large pan with cooking spray and add the chicken and rice. Cook over a low heat for 2-3 minutes, stirring, until the rice looks translucent, but not brown.

2 Add the spring onions and garlic. Cook gently for another minute, stirring frequently.

3 Pour in the wine and let it bubble up for a few minutes. Add a couple of ladlefuls of stock. Stir well, then cook over a medium heat for 20-25 minutes, gradually adding the remaining stock a ladleful at a time, until the rice is tender.

4 While the risotto cooks, remove the broad beans from their tough outer shells, then add them to the risotto. Cook for another few minutes and then season to taste, add the parmesan cheese and serve garnished with the basil leaves.

SmartPoints
9 per serving

See page 6

Balsamic roasted chicken

Serves 4

Prep time
10 minutes

Cook time
25 minutes

Whole breast fillets are roasted with peppers and onions, in a sticky balsamic vinegar sauce.

Ingredients

Calorie controlled cooking spray
4 x 150g chicken breast fillets, skinless
1 large onion, cut into thick slices
2 red peppers, deseeded and sliced into thin strips
1 green pepper, deseeded and sliced into thin strips
2 garlic cloves, crushed
4 tablespoons balsamic vinegar
100ml chicken stock, made with ¼ stock cube
Small handful fresh oregano or 1 teaspoon dried

1 Preheat the oven to 180°C, fan 160°C, gas mark 4 and mist a roasting tin with cooking spray. Put the chicken breasts in the tin and season.

2 Mist a large nonstick frying pan with cooking spray and stir-fry the onion for a few minutes, adding a little water if it starts to stick, until softened. Add the peppers and garlic, stir-fry for a further minute, then add to the roasting tin.

3 Drizzle the vinegar and stock over the chicken and veg, and sprinkle over the oregano. Roast for 20 minutes or until the chicken is cooked through. Halfway through the cooking time, spoon some of the sauce over the chicken breasts.

SmartPoints
2 per serving

See page 6

Tip
Cook 60g dried pasta, such as fusilli or penne, per person, for an additional 6 SmartPoints per serving.

Griddled chicken with herby couscous

Foil-wrapped chicken and vegetables spiced with paprika are also great for a barbecue.

Serves 4

Prep time
20 minutes + marinating

Cook time
20-25 minutes

Ingredients
4 x 165g chicken breast fillets, skinless
Juice of 2 lemons
2 teaspoons smoked paprika
1 teaspoon fresh thyme leaves, chopped
1 red onion, finely sliced
2 red peppers, deseeded and sliced
2 courgettes, cut into thin strips
Calorie controlled cooking spray

For the couscous
200g wholewheat couscous
Zest and juice of 1 lemon
250ml hot chicken stock, made with ½ stock cube
Small handful fresh mint leaves, chopped
Small handful fresh flat-leaf parsley, chopped

1 Butterfly the chicken breast fillets. Cut in half lengthways, keeping one edge attached, and open out. Cover with cling film. Using a rolling pin, flatten to a 5mm thickness. Put the chicken in a bowl with the lemon juice, paprika and thyme, then marinate in the fridge for 1 hour.

2 Take 4 large double-layered squares of foil, put a chicken breast on each and divide the vegetables between them. Drizzle over any remaining marinade, mist with cooking spray and season well. Bring the edges of the foil up and scrunch together to create a parcel.

3 Put the parcels on a griddle or nonstick pan over a medium heat, and cook for 20-25 minutes, until the chicken is cooked through and the vegetables are tender.

4 Meanwhile, put the couscous in a heatproof bowl with the zest, and pour over the stock. Leave, covered, for 10 minutes, then stir in the lemon juice and herbs. Fluff up the grains with a fork and season well. Serve the couscous topped with the chicken and vegetables.

SmartPoints
7 per serving

Chicken pies with roasted vegetables

Serves 4

Prep time
20 minutes

Cook time
55 minutes

Using filo pastry instead of shortcrust makes this pie simple to prepare and reduces the SmartPoints too.

Ingredients

200g baking potatoes, chopped into 1cm pieces
400g sweet potatoes, chopped into 1cm pieces
150g parsnips, chopped into 1cm pieces
Few sprigs fresh thyme
Few sprigs fresh rosemary
2 teaspoons olive oil
500ml chicken or vegetable gravy made with 40g gravy granules
2 x 150g chicken breast fillets, skinless, cut into small pieces
4 x 30g sheets filo pastry

1 Preheat the oven to 200°C, fan 180°C, gas mark 6. Put the potato, sweet potato, parsnips, thyme and rosemary in a large roasting tin. Drizzle with the oil and season with black pepper. Roast for 40 minutes or until tender and golden.

2 Towards the end of the cooking time, put the gravy in a large pan. Add the chicken, cover and simmer gently over a low heat for 6-8 minutes or until the chicken is cooked. Set aside.

3 Tip half the roasted vegetables into the chicken mixture. Use a potato masher to break them down, then stir through the remaining roasted veg. Spoon into 4 individual pie dishes, then top each with a scrunched-up piece of filo pastry. Bake for 10-12 minutes, or until the pastry is crisp and golden. Serve with steamed green veg such as broccoli or cabbage.

SmartPoints
11 per serving

Harissa chicken & chickpea casserole

Serves 4

Prep time
5 minutes

Cook time
40 minutes

Tender chicken thighs are gently simmered with chickpeas in a spicy tomato and onion sauce.

Ingredients

Calorie controlled cooking spray
8 x 90g chicken thigh fillets, skinless
1 red onion, finely chopped
2 garlic cloves, finely sliced
400g tin chickpeas, drained and rinsed
400g tin chopped tomatoes
150ml chicken stock, made with ½ stock cube
1 tablespoon harissa paste
Zest and juice of 1 lemon
Chopped fresh flat-leaf parsley, to garnish

1 Mist a heavy-bottomed pan with cooking spray and put over a medium heat. Add the chicken and cook for a couple of minutes on each side, until starting to colour. Remove from the pan and set aside.

2 Add the onion to the pan, and cook over a low heat for 5-6 minutes until softened but not coloured. Add the garlic and cook for a further 1-2 minutes.

3 Stir in the chickpeas, tomatoes, stock, harissa, and lemon zest and juice. Return the chicken thighs to the pan, making sure they're nestled under the sauce. Season, bring to a simmer, then cover and cook on a medium-low heat for 20-25 minutes.

4 Divide between bowls and serve seasoned to taste and garnished with the parsley.

SmartPoints
10 per serving

See page 6

Tip
For a thicker sauce, mix 1 teaspoon cornflour with some of the liquid from the pan, then stir in and simmer for a few minutes.

Chicken, mushroom & wild rice pilaf

Serves 2

Prep time
15 minutes

Cook time
40 minutes

This delicious one-pot dish of chicken, asparagus and wild rice dish is flavoured with fragrant spices.

Ingredients

2 teaspoons olive oil
200g chicken breast fillets, skinless, thickly sliced
½ onion, sliced
200g mixed mushrooms, sliced
2 garlic cloves, finely chopped
2cm piece fresh ginger, peeled and finely chopped
½ teaspoon ground turmeric
½ teaspoon ground coriander
½ teaspoon ground cumin
1 whole cinnamon stick
100g basmati and wild rice
300ml chicken stock, made with 1 stock cube
250g asparagus, trimmed and cut into 3cm-pieces
50g kale, roughly chopped
Small handful fresh flat-leaf parsley, chopped

1 Heat half the oil in a medium pan over a high heat and fry the chicken for 5 minutes or until golden. Remove from the pan and set aside. Heat the remaining oil and fry the onion and mushrooms for 5-10 minutes until softened. Add a little water if the vegetables start to stick.

2 Add the garlic, ginger and spices and cook for 1 minute, until fragrant. Stir in the rice and return the chicken to the pan. Pour in the stock and bring to a simmer. Cook for 5 minutes, then cover, turn down the heat to low and simmer for 15 minutes.

3 Meanwhile, bring a pan of water to the boil and blanch the asparagus and kale for 2 minutes. Drain, and stir into the rice, along with half of the parsley.

4 Season and serve garnished with the remaining parsley.

SmartPoints
8 per serving

See page 6

Tip
Take care not to overcook the rice – test a few grains just before the end of cooking time to see if it's ready.

Chicken, lentil & tomato bake

Serves 4

Prep time
10 minutes

Cook time
55 minutes

Toasted pine nuts add a crunchy finishing touch to this easy, Mediterranean-inspired bake.

Ingredients

Calorie controlled cooking spray
1 red onion, finely chopped
1 garlic clove, finely sliced
8 x 115g chicken thighs, skinless, boneless
250g Puy lentils, rinsed
2 x 400g tins chopped tomatoes
300ml chicken stock, made with 1 cube
Small handful fresh basil leaves
1 tablespoon pine nuts, toasted in a dry frying pan

1 Mist a large frying pan with cooking spray. Fry the onion over a medium heat for 3-4 minutes until starting to soften, then add the garlic. Fry for a further minute, then add the chicken thighs to the pan.

2 Cook the chicken for a few minutes until golden on all sides, then remove from the pan and set aside. Add the lentils, chopped tomatoes and stock to the pan. Stir well to combine.

3 Preheat the oven to 180°C, fan 160°C, gas mark 4. Transfer the chicken to an ovenproof dish and pour over the lentil and tomato mix. Cover with foil and bake for 45 minutes, until the lentils are tender and the sauce has reduced by about half. Season and serve with the basil and pine nuts scattered over.

SmartPoints
13 per serving

See page 6

Recipe index

APPLE
Chicken & vegetable traybake — 82
Chicken korma — 76
Ginger chicken, fennel & apple salad — 38
ASPARAGUS
Chicken, mushroom & wild rice pilaf — 108
Teriyaki chicken — 50
AVOCADO
Chicken taco salad — 20
Chipotle chicken club sandwich — 14

BACON
Coq au vin — 62
Balsamic roasted chicken — 100
BEANS
Chicken & broad bean risotto — 98
Chicken & cannellini bean salad — 36
Jerk chicken with Caribbean beans — 66
BEETROOT
Beetroot, chicken & orange salad — 26
BREAD
Chicken burger with blue cheese — 32
Chicken sausage panzanella — 44
Chipotle chicken club sandwich — 14
Jerk chicken with Caribbean beans — 66
Thai chicken wrap — 18
BROCCOLI
Chicken & broccoli stir-fry — 42
BULGUR WHEAT
Harissa roast chicken & bulgur wheat — 92
BUTTERNUT SQUASH
Jerk chicken with Caribbean beans — 66

CHEESE
Chicken & broad bean risotto — 98
Chicken burger with blue cheese — 32
Creamy chicken pies — 86
Goat's cheese & pesto stuffed chicken — 90
Chicken & broad bean risotto — 98
Chicken & broccoli stir-fry — 42
Chicken & cannellini bean salad — 36
Chicken & leek pie — 52
Chicken & mushroom stroganoff — 74
Chicken & vegetable traybake — 82
Chicken arrabiata — 78
Chicken burger with blue cheese — 32
Chicken Caesar pasta salad — 16
Chicken casserole with herb dumplings — 72
Chicken chow mein — 64
Chicken Florentine pasta — 58
Chicken korma — 76
Chicken laksa — 28
Chicken, lentil & tomato bake — 110
Chicken merguez meatballs — 94
Chicken, mushroom & wild rice pilaf — 108
Chicken noodle soup — 34

Chicken patties with Thai salad — 22
Chicken pies with roasted vegetables — 104
Chicken sausage panzanella — 44
Chicken taco salad — 20
Chicken tikka masala — 54
CHICKPEAS
Harissa chicken & chickpea casserole — 106
Moroccan chicken & couscous salad — 30
CHILLI
Chipotle chicken club sandwich — 14
CHORIZO
Roast chicken with chorizo & peppers — 96
Coq au vin — 62
COURGETTE
Chicken & vegetable traybake — 82
Chicken merguez meatballs — 94
Griddled chicken with herby couscous — 102
Moroccan chicken & couscous salad — 30
Paprika chicken with lentils — 84
COUSCOUS
Chicken merguez meatballs — 94
Griddled chicken with herby couscous — 102
Moroccan chicken & couscous salad — 30
Creamy chicken pies — 86
CURRY
Chicken korma — 76
Chicken tikka masala — 54
Speedy Thai green chicken curry — 60

FENNEL
Ginger chicken, fennel & apple salad — 38

Ginger chicken, fennel & apple salad — 38
Goat's cheese & pesto stuffed chicken — 90
Griddled chicken with herby couscous — 102

Harissa chicken & chickpea casserole — 106
Harissa roast chicken & bulgur wheat — 92

Jerk chicken with Caribbean beans — 66

KALE
Chicken, mushroom & wild rice pilaf — 108

LEEKS
Chicken & leek pie — 52
Chicken casserole with herb dumplings — 72
Leek & potato soup with chicken — 40
LENTILS
Chicken, lentil & tomato bake — 110
Paprika chicken with lentils — 84

MANGE TOUT
Chicken noodle soup — 34
Middle Eastern chicken with rice — 88
Moroccan chicken & couscous salad — 30

MUSHROOMS
Chicken & broccoli stir-fry 42
Chicken & mushroom stroganoff 74
Chicken, mushroom & wild rice pilaf 108
Chicken noodle soup 34
Coq au vin 62
Paprika chicken with lentils 84

NOODLES
Chicken & broccoli stir-fry 42
Chicken laksa 28
Chicken noodle soup 34
Chicken patties with Thai salad 22

OLIVES
Roast chicken with chorizo & peppers 96
ORANGE
Beetroot, chicken & orange salad 26

Paella with chicken, seafood & chorizo 70
Paprika chicken with lentils 84
PARSNIPS
Chicken pies with roasted vegetables 104
Creamy chicken pies 86
PASTA
Chicken arrabiata 78
Chicken Caesar pasta salad 16
Chicken Florentine pasta 58
PEPPERS
Balsamic roasted chicken 100
Chicken merguez meatballs 94
Chicken sausage panzanella 44
Griddled chicken with herby couscous 102
Harissa roast chicken & bulgur wheat 92
Jerk chicken with Caribbean beans 66
Moroccan chicken & couscous salad 30
Paella with chicken, seafood & chorizo 70
Roast chicken with chorizo & peppers 96
Weekday chicken & 'chips' 24
PESTO
Goat's cheese & pesto stuffed chicken 90
PIES
Chicken & leek pie 52
Chicken pies with roasted vegetables 104
Creamy chicken pies 86
POTATOES
Chicken pies with roasted vegetables 104
Creamy chicken pies 86
Leek & potato soup with chicken 40
Roast chicken with chorizo & peppers 96
Southern baked chicken 68
Ultimate zesty roast chicken 48
Weekday chicken & 'chips' 24

RICE
Chicken & broad bean risotto 98

Chicken korma 76
Chicken, mushroom & wild rice pilaf 108
Chicken tikka masala 54
Middle Eastern chicken with rice 88
Paella with chicken, seafood & chorizo 70
Speedy Thai green chicken curry 60
ROASTS
Roast chicken with chorizo & peppers 96
Ultimate zesty roast chicken 48

SALAD
Beetroot, chicken & orange salad 26
Chicken & cannellini bean salad 36
Chicken Caesar pasta salad 16
Chicken patties with Thai salad 22
Chicken sausage panzanella 44
Chicken taco salad 20
Ginger chicken, fennel & apple salad 38
Moroccan chicken & couscous salad 30
Tex-Mex chicken schnitzel 56
SEAFOOD
Paella with chicken, seafood & chorizo 70
SOUP
Chicken laksa 28
Chicken noodle soup 34
Leek & potato soup with chicken 40
Southern baked chicken 68
Speedy Thai green chicken curry 60
SPINACH
Chicken & mushroom stroganoff 74
Chicken Florentine pasta 58
Chicken noodle soup 34
Thai chicken wrap 18
STIR-FRIES
Chicken & broccoli stir-fry 42
Chicken chow mein 64
Teriyaki chicken 50
SWEET POTATOES
Chicken pies with roasted vegetables 104
Goat's cheese & pesto stuffed chicken 90
SWEETCORN
Chicken chow mein 64
Creamy chicken pies 86

Teriyaki chicken 50
Tex-Mex chicken schnitzel 56
Thai chicken wrap 18
TRAYBAKES
Balsamic roasted chicken 100
Chicken & vegetable traybake 82
Roast chicken with chorizo & peppers 96
Weekday chicken & 'chips' 24

Ultimate zesty roast chicken 48

Weekday chicken & 'chips' 24

SmartPoints index

2 SMARTPOINTS	PAGE	SERVES
Balsamic roasted chicken	100	4
Paprika chicken with lentils	84	4

3 SMARTPOINTS		
Leek & potato soup with chicken	40	4

4 SMARTPOINTS		
Ginger chicken, fennel & apple salad	38	4
Teriyaki chicken	50	4

5 SMARTPOINTS		
Ultimate zesty roast chicken	48	6
Weekday chicken & 'chips'	24	2

6 SMARTPOINTS		
Chicken & cannellini bean salad	36	2
Chicken & mushroom stroganoff	74	4
Chicken sausage panzanella	44	4
Thai chicken wrap	18	2

7 SMARTPOINTS		
Beetroot, chicken & orange salad	26	2
Chicken patties with Thai salad	22	4
Griddled chicken with herby couscous	102	4
Middle Eastern chicken with rice	88	4
Paella with chicken, seafood & chorizo	70	4

8 SMARTPOINTS		
Chicken & broccoli stir-fry	42	2
Chicken arrabiata	78	4
Chicken chow mein	64	4
Chicken merguez meatballs	94	4
Chicken, mushroom & wild rice pilaf	108	2
Harissa roast chicken & bulgur wheat	92	6
Jerk chicken with Caribbean beans	66	4
Moroccan chicken & couscous salad	30	2

9 SMARTPOINTS	PAGE	SERVES
Chicken & broad bean risotto	98	4
Chicken burger with blue cheese	32	4
Chicken Caesar pasta salad	16	4
Chicken noodle soup	34	4
Chipotle chicken club sandwich	14	1

10 SMARTPOINTS		
Chicken & leek pie	52	6
Chicken korma	76	4
Chicken taco salad	20	1
Chicken tikka masala	54	4
Coq au vin	62	4
Creamy chicken pies	86	2
Goat's cheese & pesto stuffed chicken	90	2
Harissa chicken & chickpea casserole	106	4

11 SMARTPOINT		
Chicken pies with roasted vegetables	104	4
Roast chicken with chorizo & peppers	96	4
Southern baked chicken	68	4
Tex-Mex chicken schnitzel	56	4

12 SMARTPOINTS		
Chicken & vegetable traybake	82	4
Chicken Florentine pasta	58	4
Chicken laksa	28	4
Speedy Thai green chicken curry	60	2

13 SMARTPOINTS		
Chicken casserole with herb dumplings	72	4
Chicken, lentil & tomato bake	110	4

Ultimate zesty roast chicken

Chicken burger with blue cheese

Jerk chicken with Caribbean beans

Chicken – it's versatile, nutritious, healthy and affordable, and there are plenty of tasty and exciting new ways to cook it. That's where this book from the WW Kitchen Collection comes in! With 47 fabulous chicken recipes, there's something for every occasion, whether it's a quick and easy lunch, midweek family meal or special dinner for friends. From simple soups to quick pasta dishes, classic casseroles, pies and much more, they've been created to taste great and help you lose weight. If you love chicken, this book's a must-have addition to your WW Kitchen collection.

weight watchers
SmartPoints